READING *MOBY-DICK*
and Various Other Matters

Martin Stannard

First published in the UK in 2020 by Leafe Press
www.leafepress.com

ISBN: 978-1-9999451-5-2

Acknowledgements and thanks are due to the editors of the following magazines and journals (on- and off-line) in which some of these items have previously appeared, sometimes in a slightly different form:

The Fortnightly Review, International Times, The Long Poem Magazine, M58, Misfit Magazine, Molly Bloom, Otoliths, Stride, Tears in the Fence, and *Train*

CONTENTS

View

Other Matters

READING *MOBY-DICK or The Whale*

1.

Call me optimistic. I began reading at 7.55 of the a.m.
and by 8.05 I knew that meditation and water are wedded
for ever and the next few days were to be long; they loomed
not like a snow hill in the air but like something lengthy
that begins at the beginning and will not end until you begin
to wonder about your old age and how it might be endured.
I stuffed a quick breakfast into my stomach bag, scraped
metaphorical ice from my frosted eyes, and at 8.20
was in the Spouter-Inn. By 8.30 I was abed with a man
and although I have never been abed with a man before
I have to say I have never slept better in my life. Upon waking,
p.28 was arrived and I was looking forward to 29. I calculated
that at least three or four hours must elapse before I could
resume what passes for my ordinary life, and was wondering
what might be being cooked up. Life in the street goes on
without me, but on the starboard hand of every woe there
is a sure delight: by 9.30 I was in New Bedford, a place all
beach and no background, and what is background other than
something to loafe and loiter in front of? During the morning
I travelled religion and witnessed memorials, reaching
Nantucket in time for elevenses. I had soup. By lunchtime
I was down to the ship, and my future had been told. It held
the afternoon, and further reading. (Note to self: visit
optician ASAP: I think I need new spectacles.) (Note to you:
note how I used the word *spectacles* there instead of
glasses.) And though I am mainly a stay-at-home, in my mind
I love to sail forbidden seas, and land on barbarous coasts,
and the irony of that is self-evident. Christmas came, but was
soon gone. It will never be the same again; nor will anything.

2.

Yesterday after Christmas we had to go shopping and
by the time we'd got back and had oysters and suffered
a movie I was too tired to read. It's now 8.45 a.m. today
and Limishka is still sleeping. I ascend to the deck from below
with nothing to say but a great urge to say it. I begin on
p.133 and five minutes later I have, in my own way, flowered
out in a smile. As the morning grew older by the minute
the temperature dropped degree by degree. It occurred to me
it was a long while since I had given up smoking and
I might start again—but the matter was put into abeyance
for it was time to study cetology, which I proceeded to do for
fifteen pages or so until I felt able to pass any test paper
placed before me. It was not understanding that mattered
so much as knowing. That has been well and truly
drummed into me. By lunch, by which time famishment
engulfed me, I yearned for a bite of bread, and proceeded
to table. Limishka, as is her way, had baked. Then I napped:
there was no life in me but that I had borrowed from her.
It was a quarter past five when I awoke: the afternoon was
almost past, and soon the sun would set. Dusk was imminent.

3.

I do not like to read at night. It's too dark without a light
and 185 nautical miles of page in a day is damn good going for
a landlubber. Lay up until the morrow. Limishka spent the evening
mending my braces; I sat quietly admiring her darkness skills
and laughter. A wild, mystical, sympathetical feeling was in me.
But I awoke in the mid-night (which because of exceeding
age is my wont) and, finding I needed to read a few pages of print
before I could return to sleep, picked up the book from the bed-
side table, knocking over a glass of water in the process. I found
myself at the door (watery) of the chapter (41) entitled 'Moby Dick'
—in which is retold how Ahab's leg was reaped like a blade

of grass in a field, and just about one-third of the way through
the world of this book it occurred to me how, in these days
of short attention spans and instant gratification, to attempt
such an immense enterprise would, for some, inevitably to be
torn into a quick eternity. Nevertheless, one there was
ready to take it on, sufficiently hardy not to flee from
the battle. Many are bent on quick profit; others are more
audacious and intent upon something other. But to resume:
it is the middle of the night and I am reading about the white-
ness of the whale. Beside me Limishka is, I swear, in another
country. By sunrise, by which time I had slumbered again as
the world outside the cabin window woke up, I am dreaming
of The Albatross, bleached like the skeleton of a stranded walrus.
This is not the albatross of an ancient mariner, hung about
the neck, but a vessel of long-bearded watchers, clad in skins
of beasts, torn and bepatched, standing in iron hoops, swaying
and swinging above a fathomless deep. They uttered not
a word, and in my silent sleep we parted company, and set
off again in pursuit of more dreams, more mysteries.
Had I been awake I would not have travelled so far, but still
undoubtedly have been tormented by demon phantoms. But
I was hungry, and hunger will stir from slumber even the most
determined of dreamers. A new day (page) arrived. 7.20 a.m.

4.

Coffee comes first. Then to p.285, and the matter
of portraits and pictorial delusions, curious touches, and
manifold mistakes. Consideration of teeth, of wood, of stone,
of sheet-iron, of mountains, and of the stars. And it's not
even 8 o'clock yet. The fabled heavens lay encamped
within reach of my sight, although it seems too often
are my eyes clamped closed. Does it matter if one recalls
where one comes from, or declines so to do? Perhaps that's
a line never to be crossed, or a small (imagined) death. Out
of the trunk, the branches grow; out of them, the twigs.

It's just past 9, Limishka is gone to the office, and even
though it's the morning there is supper to be planned, but
planning can always be hypotheticals put off until later.
Shall we dine on seafood? I'm not enthusiastic about that
as p.327 flows along by. Sometimes plans do not answer
at all, because something occurs that was incalculable.
In these middling waters might be seen the rare virtue
of a strong individual vitality or, on the other hand, how
hopeless it is to try to teach oneself a fine thing. Ten pages
later I am urged to ponder the utility of traditions, the law
of precedents, and the obstinate survival of old beliefs —
one's brain may be sometimes inclined to explode, there is
so much to consider and so much to know you did not know.
In the p.m. I further considered thought, and contrasting
ways of viewing what we may take for granted. It may be
an idle whim but it has always seemed to me that I read
better laid on my back than flat on my stomach, and
I wonder if anyone else feels the same way. But that is by
the by: this afternoon is darkening, storm clouds fill
the sky, and when p.385 is turned to (I have had on a head
of steam) all the lights in the room have been called upon
to perform the only task for which they exist: and my mind
is now wandering. I suppose I don't mind admitting it
was mention of the Virgin that did it, for I have a weakness,
a tendency to misunderstand, and it is time for a rest.

5.

If there is honour and glory to be found around here
I'm not sure where it is one should look. I say this apropos
of nothing much in particular other than my general
philosophy of life, which is sceptical bordering upon cynical,
and if you've been keeping track you'll see I'm progressing
at a rate of knots — around, if you can believe it, 200 pages
a day, give or take. But taking liberties with the truth is part

8

of the fun. As evening falls I light a miraculous lamp
that burns without any oil, for it is driven by electricity.
But before going any further it is important to mention
that although I am pushing on with the wind in my sails
still, we can hypothesize, even if we cannot prove
and establish, such is the subtle elasticity of that which
I treat, the more I consider this, the more do I deplore
my inability to express it, but I cannot completely make
it out, for it seems formed of thoughts and only thoughts,
dropping and dropping, but still driving on, far into
this wondrous world, as will hereafter be seen, and so
I go to bed, and sleep, and dream of schoolmasters.

6.

The allusion to sleep means that the next event will be
waking up. Some fifty years ago that would have been
in late morning but now it is just after dawn, or perhaps
just before—it's like a game of heads or tails but
the outcome is of no interest to anyone, yet there is
a reason in all things. Roses are blooming in the yard
as we arise. Good morning, sweet Limishka. I have
forgotten to say that I have nothing to say about
what might be found in the heart of what I am about.
But I have lost count of the hours that have passed
—it is a couple of days or so I have been at this—
and page 450 is here, and is in no way lamentable
(indeed, one might almost throw a party in its honour)
and we press on. We are all in the hands of the Gods,
and in the clear air of day Chapter 94, with a squeeze
of its hand, comes and goes. And had you stepped into
this room a moment ago, and had you strolled forward
nigh the sofa, pretty sure am I that you would have
scanned with no small curiosity a very handsome, to you,
and enigmatical personage, which you would have seen there,

lying along lengthwise with its feet at one end and its head
at the other, such an one as perhaps would have been
found in the secret groves of Queen Maachah in Judea —
but I digress: arrayed in decent black, occupying a couch,
intent on leaves, I read. Or I try. There is some clearing up
to do from last night but I have put that to one side for
my reading — hygiene is one thing, tidiness another,
reaching the end of a quest is something else, and at
the moment I would give an arm and a leg for this to be,
not over, but quite the opposite, over and ready to begin
again. In London, at school, I opened a copy of this
non-novel in the library and read inscribed on the fly-leaf
that one should read a page every day of one's life.
Be it set down here, I am drinking wine, and the wine
is almost gone, I pour one more glass, and this empties
the decanter. But how now, Chapter 102? Let me
take thy measure. Four and a bit pages, and on we go —
we take measurements, we age, we fossilize and call it
growing old, and shall we perish? We shall. But not yet.

7.

It being calm weather (I have neglected to mention
the time of year: it is the rainy season here: it's been raining
but now it's not. This may be information you were craving
in the Information Age.) and with a wild whimsiness, and
a not wild exclamation, availing myself of the mild, summer-
cool air that now reigns, and in preparation for the final
one hundred or so pages of this journey, I need to go
do some shopping or I shall starve, and my family along
with me. What time is it? I don't know. I've lost track for,
like the ocean, life has no discernible paths for we little men,
though for the leviathan they are as clear as highways.
Whatever — East and West, by early sun-rise, and by fall of eve,
with matted beard (I can be so uncouth!) I penetrate further
and farther and even beyond the heart of this. Learn

something. Not seldom in this life shall we be soothed,
and soothed again—but soothed only to a certain point.

8.

Not seldom in this life do we (how shall I put it) fail
to achieve that which we set out to achieve. Sometimes
I am all adroop with the business of it all. Then comes
a metaphorical breeze and my sails fill out and, for a day
or two, it's not the metaphor of a dying whale that occupies
my mind, rather it's (soothed to an even deeper gloom)
a paradoxical wondrousness unknown before. My emotions
confuse even myself, as if what I am reading is not only
not what I am living but also not what I am not even
pretending not to have not read. At night I lay by my own
side all night, seeming asleep but watching for sharks,
then the grey dawn comes on, and I slumbering arise, and
am brought back to the page—543, and less than one
hundred to go. I feel like this has been a life in words but
not in the way one is supposed to express one's self, which
is not something I have ever been able to do, and for
which I suffer every day, but not in any way that any one
can see. Here comes Chapter 118, there are so many
chapters in a life, it is hard upon high noon, I neglect to
observe the Sun because it can never tell me what I want
to know, but my whole attention is absorbed by —
by what? Sometimes it's as if a frantic old man is about
to speak, but it's not. And we live in the game, and will
die in it, and towards the evening of the day, darkness
coming on, I have lost track of the chronology here
and probably you've lost track of it too, and anyway
I wasn't trying very hard, for I cannot be that intricate.
(Bad work, bad work!) Chapter 122 is so brief it
almost does not exist, but exist it does, and we go on—
there's no need to put a musket to my head. Never mind
appearances: I've enjoyed this. So some hours after

midnight I slip through Chapter 123 and stop at 124.

9.

Next morning I pick up where I left off, over coffee
and toast and, alone at home, in an enchanted silence
but for the tumult without. I'm planning a day dedicated
to reaching the end of all that is and all that might be,
steering or being steered and all progress now determined
by ruthlessly ignoring everything else. There seems to be
a strange calm within that I trust does not prelude some
desperate scene. Some worlds must remain unknown,
and unknown worlds might empty into me, but that's
what I bought a ticket for. As if to distract me, Rachel
calls my cell several times until I turn it off. She may be
weeping for her children or just wanting a chat but
I don't care either way. And now at this time and place
after so long and wide a cruise by night and day delight
awaits to meet me: a symphony on the final day, a day
clear and steel-blue. The old man steps forth, thrusts out
his face, snuffs up the air, and sees (or perhaps not sees,
but senses) a gentle joyousness awaiting, but it is often
the case that when the day is nearly done all I am able
to consider is what was not done or, if done, done but
poorly. Today dawned fair and fresh, and a fairer day
could not have dawned, but now, at eleven in the forenoon,
the room is darkening, rain clouds fill the sky, and p.624
is arrived. You would expect there to be more to say but
all my words are spent. The drama's done. We are finished.

DESIGN AND LAYOUT

#1 (Bingo Little has gone to sleep)

Bingo Little has gone to sleep on the settee and when he wakes up
will be back in the book he came from. It's a fact there are more varieties
of jam than have been defined, described and tasted by the editors of
The Encyclopaedia of Jam. The spelling test will be held later today
as soon as all the old people have been stowed away in their little boxes
for the night. If you are cold set fire to your carpet slippers while you are
wearing them; heat rises. When it's dark we can say what we think.

There are several good reasons owls don't have fingers or toes. Typing
poems on toilet paper is a really good idea and more modern poets write
in the lavatory than you would expect. When you reach the number "129"
it's time to stop a moment to re-evaluate what it is you are doing. Bowls is
a game often overlooked from the windows of privately-owned sanatoria.
The elderly should only be microwaved in extraordinary circumstances,
such as the absence of reason, creeping inertia, and virulent dark-worm.

Things you can do on your own in bed proliferate as the years go by. One
of the best places to buy a stairlift is from a retailer who has been validated
by a select group of his or her peers and who have themselves been
validated by a similar group who have been similarly validated and so
on ad infinitum until they have all been used up and can no longer see
the mountain for the molehills. When writing letters of condolence sentences
can be short or long or medium; all that matters is you mean what you say.

#2 (For reasons not necessary to go into)

For reasons not necessary to go into football results rarely appear
in serious literature. The News is only "news" because we call it
"The News" and not "Stuff That's Happened". A message left on one's
loved one's pillow is not romantic if it's about putting out the bins. Debris
accumulation cannot be prevented by praying before you go to sleep at
night. When composing a memorandum it is diverting to remember
that the plural of memorandum is more than one memorandum.

Snow falling when combined with rain falling is known technically as
mixed precipitation and not what you might think. When your private
two-seater jet disappears in weather over the English Channel it is not
worth worrying unless you are in it. A magnifying glass just makes
your problems seem worse than they are. Your diet is not all that can
kill you. Carrots and a green vegetable look good together on the same
plate. A chef and a housekeeper will always vie for the role of "top dog".

The strange markings that appear on doors during the night are signs
of visitation by lieutenants of the Lord of Darkness. One should only visit
a therapist when all other options (including suicide) have been exhausted.
Before shelves were invented in the 14th century people kept their books
and food jars and fears in compartments of the imagination. Fruit has
magical powers that have barely begun to be properly investigated. More
than spiders live in the shadows and inaccessible corners below the stairs.

#3 (Spots on the brain pan)

Spots on the brain pan may have their origin in adolescent trauma
or too much gloom. A wicker cage cannot be guaranteed to satisfactorily
rein in the larger wild spirit. Parental understanding is sometimes
delivered too late to be of any use and can be expensive. Quotations from
Michel de Montaigne in answer to enquiries regarding one's prospects
of career advancement are unlikely to be greeted with anything other
than disdain. If there is egg on your tie people will know you as a sloven.

The collecting of different types of failure is not a calling. Condescension
is usually unattractive to potential sex partners. There can be too much advice
tapping at the plexiglass windows of the shack. Disappointment comes in all
shapes and sizes these days and fast food is sometimes quite slow. It is possible
that the missing piece of the puzzle will pop up later when least expected.
Even the smallest of dwellings can be found to be concealing unrequited love.
Indolence profits no-one. That the two-toed sloth has three toes is a mere detail.

It is alright to lay awake all night fretting if the following day is free of crucial
meetings that could change the course of your life. The instant message is no way
to say Goodbye. The blossom of the flowering plum symbolizes perseverance
and hope and is best enjoyed seen against a backdrop of snow. Some courses
of action will be more promising than others. It is essential that one respects
the difference between creeds and genres and does not cross any red lines
that have been drawn in the sand. The cavalry will be along in due course.

#4 (The difference between)

The difference between a hippo and a Zippo™ is obvious to even to the most casual observer. Starting the day with a joke is not always humanly possible but it's good if you can. It is not alright to be named after a particularly virulent form of bacterial invasion but some things are unavoidable. The ice on the top of your head will not always be there. A thawing of relations between foes is always nice as is the caress of fairy fingers during one's dreams. The arrival of the bin men spoils our peace and quiet but they are soon departed.

A sip of Buck's Fizz goes down well in the sunshine and should be followed by more sips until it's all gone. Crows have been known to glow in the dark although some facts are only true for a period of time so short it's almost impossible to measure with existing instrumentation. A green banana will become a black banana given enough time. The development of a strategy is not always something that goes to plan. One politically correct person's version of events may not always go down well at the Working Men's Club.

To have one's vision obscured by fog is to be having an ordinary day. Elderly machinery does not enjoy Winter but is determined to endure. The price of fuel threatens to go through the roof even though some people do not have a roof. Sometimes you need to talk to someone. The annual trip back home to see the family always brings with it a dose of emotional distress. Modern technology comes with its advantages and disadvantages but at least it helps us stay in touch. And you know a hippo is heavy but a Zippo™ is a little lighter.

#5 (Once the stash is satisfactorily secretly stashed)

Once the stash is satisfactorily secretly stashed leave it well alone
and practice some restraint. Mrs. Baxter is a splendid role model
for the children. Grace in a Charm Hat. Hide-and-seek among the
gravestones passes the time while some rituals are being sleepwalked.
When you say "turtleshell " you probably mean "tortoiseshell" but
it's an easy mistake to make. In your absence you will be missed.
The way the flowers are arranged suggests the presence of thought.

Enjoy your outsider status because it's all you are ever going to
have. Righteousness has changed its meaning over the centuries but
that doesn't mean it has lost all meaning. Some people will like you and
some people won't. The sun is lovely when it illuminates your darker
thoughts. Be hidden in plain sight. Good fortune comes to those who
are disdainful of the fashionable mob. Keep the things you know
close to your chest or somewhere no-one would ever think to look.

Floating scented candles can lend a sense of graciousness to even
the meanest of ornamental ponds. At funerals be careful not to sprain
your knees. It's the whiteness of the frost bestows a seasonal beauty. If
what makes you invisible can't be seen, know to be thankful. Concealment
can be what rescues you. One look at the popular lists and it's clear
why you are not on them. Charm in a Grace Hat. It is always going to
be too late to put things right and anyway right is actually wrong.

#6 (Billie and Bobbie and Charlie and Georgie)

Billie and Bobbie and Charlie and Georgie are here. If you are having issues with gender identity and you want to talk to someone who says they care there is a number you can call. Men who lay tarmac look up at the sky roughly once every couple of hours. Statistics prove themselves. The dry cleaning is always going to be ready Thursday unless it's an especially difficult stain. Cockatoos are not as popular these days as once they were. If muscular strains are reoccurring more then usual it may be a sign of decay.

People often say that life is a bit of a mystery but that's hokum. The daily struggle to appear intelligent wears us thin. You look delightful in that dress and also not in those dungarees. Be reassured that we have your best interests at heart. The neighbours will notice the improvements you have not made to the property. Ladybirds do not hibernate but in Winter they will be slow and sleep a lot. Insecurity is the disease of our times according to the experts on Radio 4. To have the physique of a wafer suggests insufficient nutrition.

It is not a good idea to be in love with yourself so tone it down and (if you can) try to be a little more self-critical. The latest figures from the government indicate that idiocy is on the increase, and they should know. When the geese head south for the Winter they do so with a confidence one can only envy. You are almost certain to be sexually attractive to someone although it might be tricky to find out who. Do not trust any algorithm you have not personally vetted for lies or whims. If you are having any kind of a problem you are not alone.

#7 (If you are daft)

If you are daft you will probably say the wrong thing more often than
not. Some words are difficult to pronounce unless you know how and include
reveille, segue and pneumonoultramicroscopicsilicovolcanoconiosis.
To be romantic is to be doomed. Things happen then they stop happening.
The limits to the aphrodisiacal qualities of the imagination may vary. Being
unable to name anyone that is actually present does not mean love is beyond
your reach. Keep a diary of the neighbours making curious noises.

There is nothing to see but an accumulation of events. Everything can be
explained away as something else. The Wise Man has emerged from out of
the primeval slime and will probably return to it when he's had his say.
Do not keep what you know inside your chest. Refusing to speak to anyone
about anything worth speaking about is one way of not doing it. The girls
wandering past your window every afternoon do not exist. Even if the days
are growing longer it is still approaching the autumn and winter of your life.

If you resemble a coal miner with light radiating from his brow perhaps there is
hope yet. Don't worry if there's less than one person in the world to whom you can
open your heart. Other people are not everything. A stretch of the imagination
is worth more than two of anything else. Next time you are in the greengrocer's
check to see if the Conference pears are talking to one another. If there is anything
more boring than mowing the lawn it has not yet been discovered. It is never too
late to be a clown. Make it known you are available for children's parties.

#8 (Loss of demeanour)

Loss of demeanour may be occasioned by plunging unexpectedly into icy mountain torrents. The farmer has taken the hackney to market, his wife riding pillion. Private discussions regarding one's marital affairs should be undertaken out of earshot of the help. It is not always possible for there to be universal approval of a new colour scheme. A calming influence may blow in from the vicinity of the room where Miranda does her aromatherapy. You have to admit that a strong infusion of Spanish blood would account for a fiery nature.

Both male and female are hardy in constitution and thrive on what is in reality poor fare. Austerity has hit the Ponderosa family pretty hard. A chest of drawers can be easily and cheaply renovated using very basic tools and cheap paint if it is not "too far gone". Admiration for workmanship and integrity will never vanish completely from the world. Home comforts should be bottled and stored with the pickled onions and other preserves. The housekeepers of antiquity knew their stuff and would gladden your eyes with their reliable dust-free cleanliness.

Everything new either changes or falls into disuse. We would all love to have more storage space because life is better with storage. The domestic was once very familiar and in the past a detailed description would not have been needed. What is meant today by "modern" is a question that arises. You have to have confidence in your own stupid ideas. Be placid if that's your nature; be friendly if that is your characteristic approach; unbridled aggression is something of which you need not be ashamed but it's best if you can keep it under wraps.

#9 (Be comfortable)

Be comfortable inside your head. One can always enjoy feathers, except when they sprout from a loved one's limbs. It's a truism that it's unpleasant to be seen in public with a Band Aid on your nose. Some people may try to enter the house through the wall but some people are unwelcome visitors. Sitting alone by the fireside ill becomes the head of a once overflowing family. Entanglement with sociological appropriateness often helps to eliminate the need for any action. A mighty iron machine designed to repel enemies will help prevent stagnation and ordinariness.

Time and its Miserable Inevitability is not a cheery title for a book, or even an audiobook. If lunchtime is approaching you can go and eat and read the rest of this later. The sound of wheels retreating through fog resonates with a surprisingly large number of people. Hypersensitivity implies, of course, inaccurate perceptions, as consciousness is fooled by inaccurate data. Sometimes you will hear something you can't see. Boys and girls are occasionally made of glass. There are worse things to do than follow one's meandering thoughts.

The goat it was that chewed your gloves. Have nothing to do with this world, only with the other. So much of what we think is motivated by anxiety. Desolate moors are symbolic of the mind's desolation so give them a wide berth. Take care of yourself. "Little's Liniment Limbers Up the Legs." It is nice when someone says your beauty is stamped on everything they see. The NHS walk-in centre is quite a long way away and is usually overflowing with the infirm. Do not be shy, and don't be afraid to say Hi! to a stranger. You know what they say about opportunity.

#10 (Soft and fluffy and welcoming worlds)

Soft and fluffy and welcoming worlds are available if you can be bothered
to go look for them. Lost souls spend all their time complaining about being
in a place "where messages refuse to send". One often says something
that sounds more perceptive than it really is. A common failing of folk is to not
recognize the flaky nature of the position they think they occupy. The sector
of the probability landscape bounded by all other possibilities and which is
therefore understandably resigned to the idea of loss now has its own app.

Boys are dumping girls and girls are dumping boys every single minute of
the day in this world and the next. Endless love comes these days with a health
warning. Deckchairs are one of life's many complicated facts and may cause
problems. "We call forth our own ends." One sometimes senses a struggle for
stylistic autonomy within The Creator's so-called range. Nearing the oceanside
it is sensible to admit there need not be much in the way of a flowing narrative
anywhere close by. One might rely on "mood" but "mood" is very unreliable.

Nobody on earth should eat a rabbit's head but some people are tucking in to
rabbit heads. "Vegan Revitalizing Cream", whatever that is, does not guarantee
the recovery of lost youth. One often hears other people claiming to have
experienced "the other". Some things have to be believed to really be seen.
When asked to accept an alternative, think thrice, and consider carefully. The
collapsation of the partition between representation and the symbolic reminds
us how abstraction is. Hang around: something wonderful is sure to happen.

#11 (This sentence has been redacted)

This sentence has been redacted for privacy. One does not often come across a person purporting to be speaking on behalf of the falling leaf. Any other interpretation of the events you're fretting about seems unlikely. One's eyes can become weary from all the looking they do. You will never be able to fully understand "the elephant ground". Scour the scenery in search of The Suspicion. Make a list of all that seems poignant. A lot has been scrubbed from the industrial landscape. This sentence has been redacted for privacy.

Rain is weather and windy is also weather and together they form another weather. A plank of wood can be a total life-saver in certain circumstances. It is perfectly acceptable to be in two places at the same time. To mimic a parrot is to ape it. To learn something "parrot fashion" is to bedeck oneself with colourful plumage that is not your own. Wyomin' is the only U.S. state whose name ends with a G. One of the benefits of a private education is that nobody needs to know what you have not learned or how much it cost.

This sentence has been redacted for privacy. Your name and address is an expression of nothing in particular but it's wise to encrypt it. The best advice coming in from around the globe is to not take any notice of advice if only because those dishing most of it out seem to be a bunch of losers. One million elephants have an enormous number of secrets. The Suspect has been concealed for safety's sake. Autumn is a season during which melancholy prevails. Choose who to talk to and be firm about it. This sentence has been redacted for privacy.

#12 (Atmosphere is not everything)

Atmosphere is not everything but it's quite a lot of it. Possibly "the best bits" have been highlighted, as if anyone can ever be a reasonable arbiter of "the best bits". Daffodils are good but the yellow has a relatively short life. One always looks for the most rewarding option in whatever it is one is involved with at the time, but whether it's possible to be sure, well, it's not really possible to know. At the moment there are nine down and one to go, but it's not what you would call cricket. A final decision is probably pending.

Old stuff has within it a certain residual value. Messages received while you are asleep might be (a) important, (b) sent from an absent love, or (b) mis-directed. Try to decide early on in your life which colour (yellow?) you like best, and never change your mind. The solitary life has quite a lot going for it, but it doesn't have everything going for it. Of all options available, the healthy one is not always the most enjoyable. Having checked the rota, it turns out that (once again) your favourite mount is unavailable.

Here comes another chapter of the adventure, and the audience is teetering on the edge of its precipice. All options are on the table top. There is more than one kind of bulb in the world, and the trickery of language can lead to all kinds of confusion and misunderstanding. One has to admire the he or the she who is able to decipher the most convoluted of codes. Psychology plays a large part in one's approach to a conundrum. When it comes to playing favourites, one could do much worse than put one's shirt on the pretty one.

#13 (One should attempt gymnastics)

One should attempt gymnastics only under professional supervision. A tower shaped like a penis casts a shadow, although its length varies from impressive to barely worth a second glance. To serenade a ladybird is to be taking one's romantic worldview to absurd levels. It might be worth trying to locate the source of your continuing enjoyment of and obsession with the tartan skirt and the knee sock but, come to think of it, it likely won't get you anywhere. Do not share what you are thinking with fellow passengers on the bus or train.

Most people talk far too much and too often. Having been found languishing upon its back the ladybug was rescued by the strolling player. To claim one does not mind another person's shortcomings would be disingenuous. Having one's parents living close to the marital home has its advantages and its disadvantages. To bend over backwards to accommodate other people is not always a good idea. It is no blessing to be at sixes and sevens with oneself. It would be refreshing to admit that the only kind of opposite sex one likes is the kind that doesn't exist.

A surrogate sister may possess a kind of satisfying but senseless quality. Desiring to dine at the intimate place settings of an angel really doesn't single you out from the crowd. The ashtray needs emptying, and all the garbage. A life apart is better than no life at all. It's no matter that strings arrive and imbue the courtyard with their soothing ointment. The only one who can speak about "belonging" is he or she who knows what it is to not belong. Please bring a cake next time you call, but what is really needed is some kind of helpful signpost. We love we.

#14 (The Cosy Nook)

The Cosy Nook Hotel stands apart from all the other genteel hostelries that grace the resort of Felixstowe-by-the-Sea. Petula's hat has evidently been designed by someone with a long career in the umbrella industry. Manacles add a touch of authenticity to any display. When the tequila and rum finally run out it will be time to begin composing one's Last Will and Testament. It might not be possible to transport your parents' house into the modern world but it's worth bringing in the boys to give it a shot.

When handing a beggar a couple of coins try not to imagine him as, for example, the escaped convict Delaney. The man in the pet shop says he can probably get hold of a parrot "for a price". There's nothing like the smell of fresh bread, or a burning bakery. Babies should be tightly strapped into a safety seat when travelling to and from college. It is rumoured that what is now a popular "House of Pleasure" was once a funeral parlour. Never forget what happened to the fish. When the wind blows you can hear for miles.

It can be pleasant to be married to the sea. If you can be bothered to open your eyes you will be able to see the new Aldi rising from the ashes of the old Roxy Cinema. The mirror may seem to have a life, and even a will, of its own, but you look good in the lederhosen. Laughter is undoubtedly the best medicine and Rex is no ordinary dog. One should try to be more open-minded about how to behave in restaurants, because social mores change over time. Retirement to a seaside cottage is an attractive option.

#15 (You can live in one place)

You can live in one place and have everything, or that's what they say. Sitting on a bare plank holding your head in your hands perhaps signifies you don't get out enough. To be deaf to the conflab and mayhem is another method of navigating the days and nights. If noise has to exist, let it be at a great distance. If equals are added to equals then the wholes are equal. To be told what we already know, that is enough, and when the plane arrives late or on time it will be here.

When barns burn they do so alliteratively, with more than a hint of danger. Science is endlessly fascinating. If equals are subtracted from equals then the remainders are equal. To be nine feet tall, that would be too tall for comfort, so be satisfied with your pet dwarf. The light is not very good here, but it will soon be the crack of dawn. When trees come into range it will be seen how they symbolize all that has never been achieved by mankind, but don't let it get you down. Nature goes on.

Beyond the window is a motorcycle and a man on it looking much more of a man than you could ever hope to be. It feels wrong to be cynical and so dismissive all the time but it also makes a lot of sense. The whole is greater than the part, which is an axiom. Self-image is something to think about but it should not keep one awake at night. Pleasure melts in the sun, and so should be enjoyed while it lasts, even if it is only fleeting, while professional coquetry may enhance a dull afternoon at the beach.

#16 (If emptiness beckons)

If emptiness beckons from the window of a tent in a sun-drenched desert and vultures perch in the clouds, go somewhere else. To venture beyond fences is to believe that life need not be as dull as it seems. Phials of tears on a bedroom dressing table are testament to broken dreams. Gender-neutral nightwear is the stuff of nightmares. If visitors visit the house when you are away on a speaking tour of foreign lands they may attempt to gain entry by smashing stereotypes. Notify your parents if you intend to change your name.

The House of a Thousand Cuts is currently closed for refurbishment and repairs. When standing before a mirror don't forget that it is also possible to stand after it, but it takes real determination. If one is experiencing a run of bad luck it will probably prey on one's mind and spoil some things. When planning to go to the other side of the world to start a new life don't forget to sell off all your livestock before you go. Footnotes and citations have their place, but in real life marzipan and raisins are much better. Some wood does not look like it.

Sky is great even when it's only "pretty good". When you look at a thing don't assume that other people are (a) also looking at it or (b) if they are, that they are seeing the same as you. Cheap wine cannot always be trusted. If sand has blown into your eyes be aware that rubbing them may cause terrible damage to the scenery. Do not deprive yourself of sleep. Do not indulge in too many days full of chemicals. If you have visions you might want to check out if they have any commercial potential. Lots of people are susceptible to the lure of the unknown.

#17 (Counting bits of hay)

Counting bits of hay is one way of passing the time in the countryside; counting sheep might just send you to sleep, so is probably best avoided. The giraffe was voted favourite wild animal by The Royal Society of Dwarfs back in the days when there was a The Royal Society of Dwarfs. The past is just one of the things you can never hope to get back. If it doesn't rain soon those "global warming" people will really think they're on to a winner. Seasons come and go but out there on the ranch it's mend the fences, dig the ditches, go look for all the stray sheep and sleep.

One way of not forgetting "things to do" is to make a note of them on the back of your hand in indelible ink. Farming on the moon is not much more than a pipe dream, apparently. If you stand far enough away from the horizon it's almost as if the infinite is coming into view. You were never meant to understand "The Great Work". It's not easy to know if God exists or not, and even if he or she or it does then who knows quite what version of God is "up there". It's been a very nice day today except for the all the accidents. In case of rain, slip a gamp into your bag.

The white rhino is not seen very often in the English countryside, which is perhaps a good thing. You can spy a tornado coming from a long away; typhoons, on the other hand, can only be forecast, and make their presence known when they arrive. It must be great to be so tall that you can look down upon everyone at concerts and political rallies. One can tell that the ice caps are melting because at the seaside there is more sea than there used to be. Sometimes you don't have to be a detective to know things don't always add up. Life can often look different from the top of the hill.

#18 (To perch upon the corner of the desk)

To perch upon the corner of the desk is not to be as a bird perched upon
a bough. Something silly is something soapy perhaps. Nothing takes very
long if you're quick about it. Don't wear that hat in here, it will scare the
girls away. Nothing can be described accurately as "cutting edge" in this
The Age of the Abysmally Blunt. You may have been born in snow but that
need not mean you always have to be seeking out Ice Maidens. Blossom
falls from the tree and blows away in the wind. Sometimes there is no air.

The candidate is too ugly to be taken seriously but vote for him anyway
because they have not yet finished constructing the alternative, and potential
is as bad as repellent. Young daffodils can take your mind off all this. When
Age begins to worry you by being "too close for comfort" imagine you are
an experiment that almost worked. It is not as cold or as hot as you think.
Having decided to spend most of your time in quiet contemplation of life's
mysteries don't be surprised if one day you wake up in fog that will not clear.

If you can't be debonair all the time at least keep your feathers clean. Symmetry
is not your enemy. Lean out of the window with your cigarette or blow the smoke
up the chimney. Organisational skills may be a natural gift or may be learned.
It's alright to obey the rules set by "the Party" but don't forget that once upon
a time you had a mind of your own. The landlord takes his time about almost
everything. A list of the most popular positions in which to watch the world
means nothing if it does not include "with one's head in the lap of Venus".

#19 (The glass you use)

The glass you use when combing your golden locks appears to be reflecting a bemused head. If you have only come here for the view take particular note of the fluting at the coast where traces of microbe culture are discernible to the truly observant. The rewards of spare-time writing can be very substantial. Wrap your legs around *The Philosophy of Modern Art* and thrust as if you are determined to somehow force your way inside it. Before submitting to the pressures of life consider what it means to live as if you don't give a damn.

On a clear day you can just about make out why you came. When you decide to delete certain unsavoury photos from your phone try to do so without a sense of guilt. In the late afternoon sunshine all the old people of the neighbourhood come out to play. Writing is the most fascinating and stimulating of hobbies. If you have only come here to make fun of the inhabitants take particular note of the stunted one-legged deaf-in-one-eye mixed-race gender-indeterminate mute who runs the Bridge Club. Vaccination against flying bacteria is advised.

To be awake is to be faced with an endless supply of questions. Be sure to renew your membership before it's too late and all the entrances and exits are blocked off. If you have only come here to fill a void then you should leave now and make way for fresh talent. The modern approach to carving out some kind of space for oneself may strike one as too selfish and uncaring but life is no picnic. Hushed conversations suggest something is building. Holding up a mirror to what's going on around may or may not provide some answers.

#20 (It may be that stray animals are attracted to you)

It may be that stray animals are attracted to you because you remind them of mother. One's self-portrait should always tell at least some of the truth. Snow falling in the months of summer would have a kind of rare beauty should it ever occur. Make the world your home. The public aviary, with its variety and seeming endless range of colour and song, depends upon all of us for financial support. It would be interesting to know what the flowers think. When you were young and fanciful perhaps the days were longer. It is impossible to know.

Can you write? Are you hungry? Did the sunlight disturb you? Can you read anything more substantial than the sports pages of a newspaper? Does the cult of celebrity annoy you? Do you love animals? Is Art of importance in your life? Will you ever have a place you can truly call home? Are birds a threat? Have you forgotten what it is to be young? Can money ever be a satisfactory substitute for love? Has your landlord forgotten you? What is the point of waking up in the morning? Do you have enough supplies in the cupboard in case War breaks out?

It is impossible to know everything. There can be no substitute for the love and caring touch of a charitable institution. Peace is a possibility but not a likelihood. When your youth disappears you will probably disappear with it, or not, as the case may be. The sky is full of a lot of things, some of which you can breathe, some of which are breathing. Make a home and call it a nest, it's perfectly alright to value comfort highly. When the weather improves go out and get some fresh air. Examine yourself closely but do not be too critical of what your eyes see.

STILL HERE

6.

When I was fourteen I joined a cycling club and at weekends would thoroughly enjoy our long excursions into the countryside, for at the time I was also a keen ornithologist. I was surprised when Jed said he wanted to join us, because he was never really the athletic type. He explained his interest lay in the relationship between girls and the bicycle saddle. I was not at all sure about nominating Jed for membership on this basis: we considered ourselves an elite club who took our riding seriously, and Jed did not even have his own bicycle, but planned on borrowing his dad's, which he'd had since the final episode of World War II. Jed's plans collapsed when his dad heard about them and decided he wanted to join us too, and they could not both use the same bicycle. In the end neither of them joined. But what Jed had said stuck in my mind, and two weeks later I was expelled from the club for what they termed "riding without due care and attention". I think they were wrong about the attention bit.

12.

I had often overheard men talking about how they found women's purses interesting but I had never understood the attraction. Eager to investigate, I asked Coco, a friend of my sister, if she would help me with my researches. One Tuesday when it was raining she and a few of her friends allowed me to have a look at their purses, which they kept in a room. They were nice enough, although I thought some too large and some too small, and some seemed weather-beaten, reminding me a little of the damaged purses I had seen in photographs of purses that had been damaged. But while Coco and her friends were doubtless very expert purse-persons, try as I might I found nothing to entice me into becoming an aficionado. I opened them, closed them, subjected them to varying levels of close examination, went outside and looked at them through the window, and even went so far as to purchase a cheap one of my own. The last of these events seemed to excite Coco and her friends, and even caused fractional stirrings of interest in my think-pot, but quite honestly it was a lot of faffing around for very little return.

15.

Madge in the office is a very interesting lady insofar as she acts as if she is very attractive when she isn't. I don't know how old she is: I estimate between forty and seventy. The word is she has been married several times to several men and, according to Jed, possesses a certain magic. She always wears a white blouse and black skirt, a lot of make up, and shoes with very high heels. I have seen our manager, Mr. Richards, purposely drop papers on to the floor and ask her to pick them up. Legend has it that Madge does not wear underpants, and a jackpot of £100 is on offer to the first person to categorically prove or disprove the thesis. During my first week, and being a practical chap, one day I asked Madge if she was wearing underpants, and she called me a sweet boy, then led me into the stockroom where she picked up a hammer off the shelf and smacked me round the side of the head. I was hospitalized for a week, and no longer care what Madge wears.

17.

While I have never thought overmuch about the work-boots of the women at the workshop, I am always happy when it rains and they don galoshes while bringing in the gimbal mountings from the delivery lorries. Even a wizened witch like Mother Gibson can be enchantment personified and mesmerizing as she splishes and splashes with her colleagues through the puddles, each balancing a crate upon their back, and their galoshes gleaming wetly through the otherwise gloom. The glistening rubber entrances the eye and brings a warm rush of blood to my happiness department. For most of my imbecile adolescence and stupid young manhood I had been merely a latent flap-eye as regards such footwear, but an encounter with an intern who claimed her name was Felicity led me to see that the traditional rubber galosh could, if viewed with the correct amount of discernment, gift a gentleman several hours of aesthetic pleasure bordering upon physical joy. I might also say here, while we are on the subject, that I own two pairs of rubber galoshes although I have never worn them in the rain. Indeed, I do not wish to wear them. I simply enjoy them for what they are.

21.

I shall never forget the first time I went to work wearing one of my sister's trapeze dresses instead of my own goose feather-lined waistcoat. It was a Monday. The weather had been a little inclement of late but that morning was quite warm and pleasant, with only a 5% chance of precipitation predicted. I had enjoyed my usual bacon and egg and cup of tea. The newspaper had a headline about something political in Africa that I wasn't interested in, and a photograph of the Queen doing something. My mother was going on about noise from the neighbours, but there was nothing unusual about that. I caught the 7.35 bus and was at the workshop by five to eight. I had chosen one of her more exotic numbers, red with black trim and a sequined neckline, and it caressed me all day, although the lack of pockets and anywhere for my sweetmeats was a trial. I think I did not re-flange a gimbal accurately all day, I was so wary of oil spills, but Foreman Alf didn't notice, being too preoccupied with his weft-restraining conundrum, and Madge in the office having not turned in on account of lady flu.

25.

As a child I was taught not to stare at people, so I grew up not looking at people most of the time. Then one day I was shopping for man-dab powder in a department store and above me on an escalator saw a female lady dressed as what I thought was a ballerina, although it may have been a trick of the light. I was unable to force my eyes away, and then she reached the next floor and disappeared among a bewildering array of feminine secrecy items. That evening in bed I replayed those few seconds over and over again in my mind and tossed and turned so energetically with wakefulness that the elves on my shelves vibrated sufficient to tumble to the floor and provoke irritating warbles of enquiry from my downstairs parents. From that day to this I have looked more closely than others might at what women wear, so much so that I have developed a slight hunch, and a crick in the neck and shoulders from all the stooping, twisting, and squeezing into tight corners my interest necessitates. My physiotherapist says I will probably be like this the rest of my life, and he is probably right.

THAT THING

We once had one in our house
with handles on both sides. But
I forget its name. Sometimes

I even forget my own. The self is
an overlaying of multiple identities,
comprised not just of what is

remembered and forgotten, but
of how one is located in the wider
questions of belonging, memory

and solidarity. At least, that is what
was on my mind as I lit a bonfire
in the kitchen, which is where

I was located. It's a mystery as to
what that lump is but the chances
are it's nothing to be concerned

about. There are better reasons
to lay awake at night worrying
yourself sick. I am from here,

I thought, and recognise the pots
and pans, and how if one polishes
them enough they shine like brilliant

household suns. I think I may go
and live in a shed when all this is
over. In the last twenty years

average house prices have grown
about seven times faster than
average income. That's on my mind

as I write this, and watch the fire
brigade go about their business
with consummate professionalism

and gusto. It occurred to me also
that Galileo said "Nature's great
book is written in mathematical

symbols", although I think he said it
in Italian and it's not really relevant.
It's interesting what crosses one's

mind as the events of the day occur,
watched by miserable youths and
unquiet presences who, with nothing

to do but act as reminders of what
has been lost, refuse to stay home,
and instead nibble away at the edges

of what would otherwise be a perfectly
acceptable existence. Here comes
another little person trying to attract

my attention. Take my hat, please.
You'll see it's not been keeping much
warm at all. Those are shadows

taking shape before my very eyes,
and that's a horror show over
there, and those little horror shows

gathered around them will, I guess,
be their children. How awful!
The boys and girls I have known,

the workmen and the labourers
on the estate, they are in the past
now, of course, but they are still

kind of present, although I don't
know their names, and never
did. And when old Chivers choked

on a chicken leg everyone thought
it was a joke until it was too late.
That was a learning experience for

all of us, and is on my mind as
I write this. The burning issues of
the day are ablaze with themselves

but grow tiresome. To be a fireman is
apparently the career of choice among
an increasing number of university

graduates, and is a sign of the times.
Yes, thank you - I will have another
of those canapés. They're delicious

even if they're not home-made.
And thank you for reading this.
You've made my life better, briefly.

LET ME ASK YOU THIS

Do you think I ask too many questions? Do you?
Is curiosity one of my more charming traits? Isn't it
rather inquisitiveness? Is there a difference? Does
it matter? Whatever you may choose to call it
do you find it extremely annoying? Am I annoying?
Is the world as a whole somewhat annoying?
Are the people in the world, in general, annoying?
Or is it you are too easily annoyed? Is your annoyance
justifiable? Are you suited to where you find yourself
in the world? Would you be happier somewhere else?
Or as someone else? Is your skin a good fit?
Are you at peace with your thoughts?
Do you think you are a good role model for your
children? Are you sure they are your children?
Do they look like you or behave in ways
that seem to have been learned from you? Do
your children like you? Are you sure? Does it
sometimes feel that what you once knew to be
certainties have now put on a cloak of doubt?
Are you sure that what you think is doubt is not
just a new certainty you are afraid to acknowledge?
Does the prevalence of paradox in life bother you?
Is what you think paradox what you think it is? And
if what you thought to be uncertainties prove
only to be certainties in disguise can you be sure
of anything? Are you sure of your reflection in
the mirror? Is the mirror trustworthy? Are your eyes?
Can you believe them, or your ears? Can you
believe anything people say? Can I believe anything
you say? Do we give away our trust too easily?
Do you think I'm unsociable? Should I get out more?
Do you think I read too many books?
When I say I don't like most people do you think
I'm being unreasonable? Or do you think

I'm joking? Do I make you laugh? Do you think
I'm sometimes too serious or sometimes not serious
enough? When you say I'm wise are you saying it
to make me feel good about myself? Do you think I feel
good about myself? Do you really think I'm wise,
or just pretending to be wise? Does wisdom come with
age? What's the difference between wisdom
and not having the patience to tolerate other people's
nonsense? Is tolerance another name for surrender?
Is surrender a way of getting through the day?
Which is easier: getting through the day or through
the night? Is a surfeit of bad dreams anything
to worry about? Do dreams ever come true?
What's the difference between dream and fantasy?
Is it possible to have too much imagination?
Can imagination take up too much space in the house
and exclude reality? Shall I bother to ask what we mean
when we say "reality"? Is my reality different from yours?
Do you think I take everything too much to heart?
Do you think I'm talking about me or about you?
Do you think I'm talking about me or you or someone
else? Does it matter? Is self-questioning an admirable trait
or is it potentially self-destructive? Is therapy an option?
Have you ever known anyone come out the other end
of therapy a better person? Isn't it better to get drunk
with the man or woman you love and thank God for
them? But isn't love something of a minefield? Isn't love,
to use another metaphor, the garden where self-
deception flourishes? Or is love simply a mystery,
a puzzle beyond any possibility of solving? Are
our problems too many? Would it be better to forget
about the problems and make the most of the day?
The days fly by, don't they? So they can't be pigs,
can they? Or can they? Do you sometimes think

there are not enough hours in the day? Some days
do you lay abed in the morning and refuse to get up?
Do you not see the point? Do you see the point
of my asking you if you don't see the point?

PRECES: CONTEMPLATING MRS. BAXTER

Versicle:	It is not we who choose to awaken ourselves.
Response:	Mrs. Baxter chooses to awaken us.
Versicle:	How are we to know the will of Mrs. Baxter?
Response:	She leaves notes on the fridge door. That's one way.
Versicle:	This is a country whose centre is everywhere and whose circumference is nowhere.
Response:	We do not find Mrs. Baxter by travelling but by standing still.
Versicle:	In Mrs. Baxter you find that perfect humility and perfect integrity coincide, and Hell is where there is no Mrs. Baxter.
Response:	You can say that again!
Versicle:	Some pleasures may not be renounced.
Response:	A shopping trolley gives glory to Mrs. Baxter by being a shopping trolley.
Versicle:	Let our tongues taste no bread that does not strengthen us to praise Mrs. Baxter.
Response:	Let our tongues get at her cakes too!
Versicle:	Mrs. Baxter demands close attention to reality at every moment as she reveals herself in the mystery of each new situation.
Response:	Sometimes she'll get a last-minute appointment at the clinic if there's been a cancellation.
Versicle:	You may think you can live without Mrs. Baxter but you can't.
Response:	There can be no contemplation of domestic peace where there is no Mrs. Baxter.
Versicle:	Those who try to escape from an attachment to their illusory self by treating the good things of Mrs. Baxter as evil are only confirming themselves in a terrible illusion.
Response:	For sure! Have they never tasted her dumplings?

Versicle:	No man who simply eats and drinks whenever he feels like eating and drinking, who smokes whenever he feels the urge to light a cigarette, who gratifies his curiosity and sensuality whenever they are stimulated, can consider himself as not needing Mrs. Baxter.
Response:	When you and I become what we are really meant to be we will discover not only that we love one another perfectly, but that we are both living our life in the image of Mrs. Baxter.
Versicle:	Keep your eyes clean and your ears quiet and your mind serene.
Response:	Breathe the air Mrs. Baxter breathes.
Versicle:	To be unknown of Mrs. Baxter is altogether too much privacy.
Response:	We're not sure what this means, but we agree anyway!
Versicle:	It is good to wait in silence for the home-baked tarts Mrs. Baxter brings.
Response:	As soon as you have tasted one you will want another.
Versicle:	Every one of us is shadowed by Mrs. Baxter.
Response:	She is the woman you want her to be but who probably cannot exist.
Versicle:	Some alleged men, and a few so-called women, think Mrs. Baxter is a creation intended to exorcise feelings of guilt about poor housekeeping.
Response:	Every one of us has an idea of Mrs. Baxter that is limited and incomplete.
Versicle:	Flight from the world is nothing else but flight from Mrs. Baxter.
Response:	In order to find Mrs. Baxter one must go out of oneself.
Versicle:	As a magnifying glass concentrates the rays of the Sun into a little burning knot of heat that can set fire to a dry leaf, so Mrs. Baxter gets the housework done.
Response:	Mrs. Baxter will be here at 10, as usual.

VIEW

VIEW #1
The Distant Lights

Snow is falling but is already melting before it
hits the ground. It seems like a lifetime since last
we traded opinions concerning the quality of
our respective behaviours. "Heaven abandoned us

like an aborted world". Your lashes flicker in the usual
coquettish manner and it's all one can do to ignore
meaning. There are many ways of saying this, but
they all add up to the same thing. If only we had

remembered to bring our sun block and other
outdoor gear. But to be ill-equipped for the world
is our default position, apparently. Trying to fix
the problem will pass the time, although there isn't

much of that. If it's true we are really over-heating
at least we'll be living nearer the beach. The livestock
have wandered off on to the moor and are at risk of
disappearing into dives. Bring ointment for the eyes.

VIEW #2
The Puzzler

The enlightened approach would be to allow
Mr. & Mrs. Everyman access to the world's treasures.
This is not going to happen. Every afternoon we go
for a walk in the park for exercise. Sleep might be

rubbish and the waking hours are not much better.
There's a pile of bricks where a pile of bricks should not
pile. It's not simply a case of opposites attract. "… and
here the first time that ever I saw women come upon

the stage." Eventually one grows tired of always being
expected to enjoy the unexpected. Yes, the food was
indigestible but that's more than the hostess will admit.
And yes, we were able to clean the carpets. A dash

of delicacy becomes the older lady or gentleman.
It is dull and grey outside in real life, but a degree of
grace is not really much to ask. It is not forthcoming.
Tonight's movie is *The Invasion of the Bee Girls.*

VIEW #3
The Voice In The Head

Once upon a time a handsome prince fell asleep on top
of a handsome princess. Is that a lark one hears singing
among the chimney stacks? And the Hungry Giant is
a figure of fear in all the villages around. The smart devices

appear to have minds of their own, and have started
making up their own excuses. To be not of this world, or
the next. One can be inclusive or exclusive, sociable
or unsociable, right or wrong. "In general, I do not draw

well with literary men: not that I dislike them, but I never
know what to say to them." Nothing requires justification
in this poem. There are always terms and conditions.
He thought he had fallen asleep upon a field of green.

That story, the explanation of why things have turned out
the way they have, it's all made up, right? It's up to you
what you believe. It's only our entire future at stake. Did
the impossible happen yet? Mmm. Oh. Aah. — Yawn etc.

VIEW #4
The Plumbing Company Ltd.

Sea levels are rising but we'll probably be safe on
this traffic island. Never mind the tap on the door — all
laments are a version of The Communal Cry. It's not much
good sitting around waiting for "vintage" or "classic"

to arrive. The afternoon's cello lesson is about to begin
and the weather — rain — complements one's rather
sombre mood. "And words like swords and thunder-clouded
creeds". Too much frivolity causes warts and boils and

pustules to break out in awkward and unspoken places.
Diversification is the name of the game these days
according to Trixie and Joy and all the staff at Lux Massage.
Mondays always seem a little bit wetter than the other

eight days of the week. Although what people do can be
explained, they also seem determined to leave you bruised
or a little bit stained. And having been once marooned
one does not wish to be marooned and alone again.

VIEW #5
The Estrangement

There are letters that should be written but there
is always a putting off. Sit still and wait for the day
you feel young and alive and healthy again. "It is true
that I can no longer remember very well the time

when we first began to know each other." Grey clouds
white clouds silver clouds driven by the March wind
race across the blue sky. Over behind the pumping station
a transparent family is living the dream. One cannot help

but wonder about "the modern way of life." Here is
a desert and here also are we, bewildered by camels.
Having always been encouraged to be true to oneself
it is impossible to feel any regret for all those much-touted

moments of honesty. Lay quietly at night and listen,
if you dare, to the darkness. The feeling of being too far
from home for ever there to be a chance of reconciliation.
When there is no-one to talk to you have to talk to yourself.

VIEW #6
The Programme

To be cold or ugly or forlorn or all four may well be
today's thing, but who knows? It's almost impossible to
keep pace with the pace of change. That Chinese
calligraphy brush is from another time and — oh, it's also

available on Amazon. We are not a small town branch of
The National Society of Trainee Creative Writing Tutors,
or are we? The best place to curl up and sleep is that little nest
of solitude you concocted for yourself. Someone likes you

but they live too far away to be of any use. "As delicate as
a bee's wing, cool as the heart of a tea-rose". The ladybirds
do not enjoy this weather; they're not built to withstand it.
Soon the Championships will begin. The excitement

is already mounting. You will be receiving a visit in the next
few days from our broad-shouldered representatives.
Relying on technology alone should not and cannot replace
the personal. Connections may not always be available.

VIEW #7
The Light and The Shade

Image is not everything, which is why one should
choose one's words carefully. Your public persona does
not interest anyone any more. "Oh sweet sound of the rain
on the ground and the roofs!" Sunshine falling upon

the white building across the way accentuates
its whiteness. Although you may be a little bit down
remember it is only work, not life. One has friends,
even if not many, but they wither in sunlight, grumble

in the yards of taverns, and litter the riverbanks.
Refuse the shadows. That is a very nice safari outfit
you are wearing. Are you off to look for elephants? A box
of books is a world to explore. Post a photo somewhere

online. There are so many things to do, but not much time
in which to do them. Unless the unexpected crops up
we will end with a joke. Husband: Can you make breakfast
in bed this morning? Wife: No, I'll have to do it in the kitchen.

VIEW #8
The Modern Artist

Someone is at the door, the neighbour probably on
the borrow again. Perfect Happiness is one condition
among many that remains unlikely. It is 11:18 a.m.
of a Wednesday and the storm is hovering on the horizon

and the music is something of a lament and one has to
push on if one is ever to reach the envisaged end,
the "target" if you will. Sing a jolly tune! but remembering
how is always difficult. It would be good if the things

one enjoyed were to arrive in more convenient packages.
But to consume an entire other person in one sitting, it's not
natural, and neither is to be held together by only Sellotape™
and willpower, though "The color-field people were a different

story." Perhaps redecorating is the answer, it would be
almost like starting afresh, as if none of this ever happened.
Or how about leaving town, disappearing in the middle of
the night? Later, watching a movie, ideas begin to take shape.

VIEW #9
The Authorized Autobiography

Things may not be great, but the last thing you want to
do is marry someone like your father. This pen reminds me
of what was intended but never occurred. There is no
temptation to try and re-fashion the past. But those were

the days, what? The "live" version of existence usually sounds
more convincing than the studio recordings, or the episodes
published in book form years after the event. It is not always
easy to look on the bright side. "Sin, is it sin whereby

men's souls are thrust into the pit?" The audience exercised
extreme tolerance and patience and although they had every
right to walk away and demand their money back they
didn't. You yawn, and every now and then the world yawns

with you. One can usually explain the source of the trouble
but occasionally it's impossible. There is a song about how
it's raining love, but it's not. The funny side has gone missing
and it would appear to be time to take a well-earned break.

VIEW #10
The Spiritual Adviser

Here comes another literary aspirant brandishing
a pencil as if they were sporting "dark lashes beating in
the scented silences". Standards don't seem to exist
anymore. A dish sits empty and alone, awaiting the arrival

of ambrosia. During the years of austerity people
still found ways to decorate themselves. Occasionally
a lady is spotted carrying a different kind of parasol.
One may find oneself in a position of authority but respect

has to be earned. Falling in love no longer answers. An air
of goodwill once graced these avenues. By the way, thanks
for supporting the cosmetics industry: the Red Goddess
lipstick suits you. If it's direction we need maybe we should

be following the example of the mist as it drifts languidly
around, there to find a method by which to relax and take
what we can find in the way of enjoyment. If you hear
a choir start up you know it's time to start worrying.

VIEW #11
The New Arrivals & Departures

Young people are catching you up but it really doesn't
matter much. "Oh no, it's his stiff back!" Before one
can arrive somewhere one has to leave somewhere
else. Travel for social and domestic purposes is unlikely

to take us out of ourselves. The night brings nightmares
and yet another new political party. Happiness comes
and goes. Sometimes the day doesn't bother to get up
in the morning. We're living in a time that hasn't been

written yet. One needs to feel safe before emerging
into the light, perhaps quietly, perhaps with a fanfare
and celebrations going on way past bedtime. Landing with
grace, the birds acknowledged the applause of the tiny

people who had waited for them in the rain. Alice had not
expected to be in a poem, then the wind whisked her away
into murky parts of town. Energy is exhausting and now
our ink is running out, so *au revoir* until we are refuelled!

VIEW #12
The Melody Maker

The day begins in a cloud hat. "My Lord told me how
the King has given him the place of the great
Wardrobe." Foreign language songs are not as popular
as once they were, yet some people insist upon

saying we have come a long way. Having written
a really catchy tune in his head he cancelled the rest
of the week. You just doodle and dawdle and it's enough
to make your fortune. But if we were all able to do that,

well, where would the challenge be? The crooked lane
stretches a crooked mile and it is not always possible to
reconcile optimism with how things pan out. Walk headlong
into the dip of doom with one's eyes closed. Deciding what

to wear to the dance is always a problem. People are
whistling, determined to be happy. Out on the village green
there is a re-enactment of something from the past when
we won. What o'clock is it? It might be too late already.

VIEW #13
The Sense of Futility

One would "love" to pass a pleasant few hours in
the English countryside before Death arrives. Pastoral
dreams, greens and browns, dried-up streams, the debris,
and the various insects. Places contain people sometimes,

which counts against them. But the other hand, upon which
things sometimes are, holds things in a very different way,
don't you think? Life happens under several headings.
There has been some ill-discipline within the ranks

of the rank and file. It's good to have one's existence
confirmed. But "I've been thinking it over and you must
NOT change that title." Suddenly all the merchants raised
their prices by about 5%. Once upon a time a little lad had

a satchel full of recipes for success. The *Selle d'Agneau aux
laitues à la Grecque* was very tasty although it is only ever
served on special occasions like a passing or another passing.
Some days there is nothing to say, so keep your mouth shut.

VIEW # 14
The Awful Truth

The Squeamish people's history, culture, societal customs,
and other knowledge has been transmitted by email from
generation to generation. Any old thought can be turned into
a species of literature. Take a sliver of whatever floats by

then inflate it until it becomes a kind of inedible pudding.
Those old men who appear to control the world (because
they do) will always be there. The citadel will only topple
if pressure is applied in the right place. "His journey to

the East had not made him more conventional." Count on
nothing until counting cannot continue, then begin all over again.
They're planning to put a plaque on his head where his brain
used to be. The librarians would be happy to allow you into

the library but unfortunately the library seems to have
disappeared. There has been a reduction in social service
expenditure by government. Sometimes you lose the will
to live. Someone suggests playing The Depression Game.

VIEW #15
The Happy Overseer

There are depths and they can be plumbed without
much effort. Oh, here comes that wet rain again,
with its associations of grief and of interminable tearing.
(How to pronounce?) "Zenith of my healing." Do not

be Beat. That's the First Commandment. Sometimes
one almost falls asleep typing. "A whole world distant,
absent, almost gone". Well, it may well be that the Prose
is superior to the Verse. It doesn't really matter what

anyone thinks, does it? Everything is disappearing
under a low cloud of blankets. They just go on and do it
anyway, because it pays. There are positions need filling,
after all. "The Wasted Years", a novel by Mr. G. Perkins.

Having applied to be a musician only to be rejected
it behoved him to take up the ~~sword~~ pen. Editors appear
to be in short supply these days. And people need so-called
friends if they're going to get ahead. Or a pea-green boat.

VIEW #16
The General Practitioner

A fever bedevils the body politic. All the furniture has been
designed to accommodate the old and the unlikely. The nurse,
from whom one has had the pleasure of receiving a variety
of inoculations, vaccinations, advice, and the occasional

instructional video, has no sense of humour. This afternoon's
'Afternoon Movie' is *Death in the Afternoon*. "Being naturally
truthful, he did not see the point of these exaggerations,
and was borne on by a natural sense of the fitting,

was indeed a great master of the art of living". With
Age comes Wisdom, and with Wisdom comes the knowledge
that one's future days of fun are very probably going to be
limited in number. As the minutes are ticked off one by

one, so one is oneself also slightly "ticked off". The truth
and a pack of lies seem to have gotten all muddled up
recently. "This is confirmation of your appointment at 15:15
on Monday Mar 4. If unable to attend please reply CANCEL."

VIEW # 17
The Vicious Circle

A whirl of thoughts. Impossible to pin anything down.
"We have had long periods of failure before. We are
having one now." Falling asleep knowing one is going to
wake up. Always that feeling of being alone, and of being

trapped inside this. Having been talking to oneself for
so long, talking to someone else is too difficult. Don't even
bother to try. Always meeting oneself coming back,
sometimes it's difficult to remember why one set out in

the first place. Something you don't really want to write
about. Possible Truth. Perhaps it's too late to do anything
other than retreat into oneself. The morning arrives
and it's another middle of the night. Some things are

impossible to let go: the scars, for instance. Eggs fallen to
the kitchen floor, the dragon eyeing the mess with interest.
As if one did not understand the basic rules of the game.
Outside it's downpouring again because it jolly well has to.

VIEW #18
The Workshop

Here we go again. Here we go yet bloody again. Please
accept our apologies, "our apologies" being a euphemism
for our having had nothing better to do. Someone is waving;
it is impossible to know to whom they are waving. "Of

nincompoops. Of professors. Of judges. Of priests. And
of Cabinet Ministers." There was a song we were trying to
remember from our youth that had more life in it than
anything we have come across in all the years since. Then

we realized we had deceived ourselves. So many stars
visible when we are asleep. Ennui, and the desire to not do,
is infectious. The seeming endless story, how it does not allow
one to think straight. Having been written many times before,

the squib self-destructed. Sitting and watching, and the world
going by without any help. And so, instead of attending your little
group and being sweet, we disappeared ourselves. But how
to make it permanent, over-arching, and all-embracing?

VIEW #19
The Long Haul

Listen up! We fucking hate you, the sound of you, the length
of you, the parameters of you, the tentacles of you, the meaning
of you and the almost certain endlessness of you. It is possible
now to understand what shame means. What is underground

does not necessarily stay underground. Minor irritations
may grow into major eruptions. "It's just the sea." And one day
one of those creatures from mythology will appear to
undermine all our certainties. If the Toblerone™ explodes

several confectioners will have egg on their face. You can go
and climb the stairs and while you're there perhaps investigate
whether or not that world has stars too. When it rains one may
easily forget so many things. Songs, sweets, etc. On the other

hand, we love the existence and the persistence of you,
the inevitability of you, the couldn't care less-ness of you. Some
people, not all people of course, appear to know everything –
but they don't. "Pond Life" (Puffin Picture Book 93) 5/-

VIEW #20
The Out of Step

If team selection doesn't matter to you, and teamwork, it's
likely you have under-estimated the challenges that lay ahead.
"What more could he have done?" If it's issues you want
addressed, please click on 'Sundries'. If you see someone

wavering, urge them to be steadfast. If everything appears
to be too nice, too polite, remember who you are. If feeling
left out is appealing, join the club. If there is less you could
be doing, don't do it. Defy yourself. If your husband or wife is

gone missing, try the "Lost & Found". Having been abandoned
by the netball team he was no longer welcome in any of
the quality High Street lingerie departments. Reduced to shopping
online for remnants of the figments of one's imagination. There,

disappearing into the distance, hurtles the cavalry, a bunch of
dudes with whom one has nothing in common beyond life, such
as it is, on earth. The time has come to hang up one's wingèd
boots. If you're a good boy someone will make you a cup of cocoa.

OTHER MATTERS

Matter No. 29 : People have taken to sitting alone, like the Sun. It is alright to sit alone like the Sun, but not all the time.

Matter No. 35 : That which cannot be perceived through the thickest of veils shall be deemed not to exist.

Matter No. 48 : It has come to our attention that on occasion a songstress has outdone the fiddle, and piped a note so thin that even a bird's throat has been incapable of uttering it. The songstress is being sought.

Matter No. 138 : Debate as to whether the soul should contain iron or stone is ongoing. The current position is that iron is better than stone, but stone is acceptable.

Matter No. 144 : Some people still rise with the Sun and set with the rising of the Moon, and others do otherwise. The review continues as papers flutter from desk to floor at the slightest nudge of a through draught.

Matter No. 188 : It remains unfortunate to be a grey-haired man sense no longer visits.

Matter No. 189 : It remains fortunate to be a grey-haired woman desirability long since abandoned but whose housekeeping skills remain undimmed.

Matter No. 192 : Maternity/Paternity vouchers are no longer redeemable, and as the eagle soars beyond the mountains so shall The Fates draw their blueprint for our future upon the ocean floor.

Matter No. 201 : The hunting of imaginary bears is permitted only between March and May, and people should hunt in pairs. No further advices on this matter will be given.

Matter No. 240 : Car parking is not permitted anywhere. Keep moving; consider returning to the horse. That's what the signs say. Read the signs.

Matter No. 274 : Someone carried off the stopper of the ink bottle in the Main Office. It is forbidden to carry off the stopper of the ink bottle in the Main Office.

Matter No. 286 : Scholars have established that in its youth the ocean used to wander between slabs of land and is now gradually being sucked up into the sky by science to become rain. School textbooks will be amended accordingly.

Matter No. 287 : It follows that rivers represent the childhood of the ocean. School textbooks will be amended accordingly.

Matter No. 300 : The recurring matter of the absence of Common Sense will no longer be considered owing to time constraints. All enquiries should be made to the Administrative Office.

Matter No. 301 : The Administrative Office is no longer located where it used to be, and its email account has been deleted.

Matter No. 302 : As part of the "Back to Nature" initiative, Information Technology matters will in future be dealt with by the farmyard animals.

Matter No. 303 : [struck from record]

Matter No. 444 : Challenges to the belief that Duty is sacred and one may not be dumb in the presence of the Law have been acknowledged and dismissed.

Matter No. 527 : The following items are forthwith subject to a 0.5% Pleasure Tax: handcuffs, pipe-cleaners, silk kerchiefs, playing cards, raisins, whips, herrings, instruments for polishing dull things, books about the planets, and gymslips.

Matter No. 531 : There is always a beautiful day guaranteed if one cares for a pet.

Matter No. 532 : All pets must be registered with the Pet Authority. (Registration fees apply.)

Matter No. 572 : Societal stasis is confirmed as "subject to appropriate adjustments."

Matter No. 599: The intricate mechanisms of government are already sufficiently complicated, yet it may become necessary they be rendered more so.

Matter No. 617: The matter of the treatment of women will be dealt with separately as stipulated in Article 396 (12/1897) of our Terms and Conditions.

"I had always felt, you know, if you got within two or three bucks of it......"
- Bob Newhart, from "Retirement Party"

4. Relishing The Mizzles

Relishing the mizzles fish cut capers on the water
Amidst the zephyry zephyr swallows askew shuttle
Umbrageous trees are teeming with captivating flowers in the vernal
The wind dies down and the wrinkling combers pacify in the vesper
On the jade steps white dews grow
Deep in the chilly nightfall into one's socks they impale
In a skiff I would totally disappear forever
When can I shed life's cumbers?

32. Wayfaring Wild Geese

Wayfaring wild geese files seem like a sewn array
I deplore being caught in the jitters on the Beach of Jitters
And stranded in desperate straits in the Desperate Straits
Totally unsettled by my doles and bogged down by official devoirs
If I've not been excruciated by the torture of the asunder disposal
I believe anyone would have his hair turned hoar under this sorrow
My chained melancholy is really unbreakable
No one is as habdab-stricken as myself

89. My Exquisite Carriage

My exquisite carriage stops for some stews visiting a mistress
The hyaline sky wave in the widespread wavering diaphanous combers
Wrings tangerines dangling from trees glittering like myriad golden lavalieres
Only insouciant people like me find this place a repair diurnal
I may as well drink to my fill the supernal's liquor whatsoever
Quaff the fluid glow where another ten ornate punters put up for the vesper
Who can have this catena of dismals uncoupled?
Whoever can snuffle the twittering orioles?

101. Descends A Devastating Belle

Descends a devastating belle from the heavens high over
Exquisite fans are uphurled as maids help her out from her silk portières
And usher her into a fragrant carriage
When she goes to tie up her espousals
In her luxurious ninefold upholstered conjugal boudoir
Cozily cozily she cozes till end of the day
There my cummerbund will be released by the pine zephyr
When we coze while trimming the candle under the west window

175. Whence The Dingles

Whence the dingles of a donned sword fade out with the recoil
On this night of rain we tattle under the protracted deluge
The woods and fields are to a desolate destitute abraded
Even cooking becomes difficult and cunctated
Just pining for lovesick is inutile
I'd rather my dismals turn into hysteroid
But by chance I'll run into a gaffer rural
And in a pleasant discourse we'll engage and forget to truce

191. From The Fragrant Osmanthus Leaves

From the fragrant osmanthus leaves the moon dews drivel
Staying clean and aloft and left to starve but still refused by any boodle defiled
High up on trees but away the cicada's chirrs are muddled
Every night on the fifth watch its chirr trails off
But the insentient tree on which it settles remains in fine fettle
My whole family is free from any boodle defiled
Don't burn out your spring yearnings with the vernal blows
Every inch of lovesick turns out into an inch of ash coal

222. Leisurely Relaxing

Leisurely relaxing natty orioles set the tempo with their entrancing twittering pulsatiles
While I watch the meadow turn viridescent in the mizzles
Listening to wheresoever the spring turtledoves coo
This is the insouciance I always aspire amidst the serene tranquil
In my present capacity this is not always available
There are devoirs I've to uphold
But relaxing insouciantly myself in the wealds
The verdant mountains cleanse my pent up dismals

244. Whence For The Mizzly Vista

Whence for the mizzly vista who'd be my vier?
All these years I've either fallen in the dumps or been ailing
So to get over my long disgruntles
And relish the sparkling vernal glamour is at odds with carpe diem of joie de vivre
I'd like to wear a blossom on my head but there is no one at my disposal
I'd also like to revel in a booze but have no boon fellows
Nobody will care even if I am sozzled
Who will come visit this man in the dumps today when he is over a barrel?

WHAT I DID AND HOW I DID IT

1. How I Coped With Living Among Morons

The day I attained adulthood I heard the flapping of wings, and a dark hawk alighted upon my left shoulder and whispered in my ear about how I ought to go my own way, and although I should make a show of liking people I had to remember it was just a show and to hold on to my true and inner self. It was something like that. I don't remember the exact words, because I was a bit distracted by having a dark hawk on my shoulder. Anyway, I took the advice, and I would reckon the success rate at 60/40, or 40/60, thus rendering the title of this paragraph questionable, whichever way you look at it.

2. How I Decided Women Were Preferable To Men

Some of my male friends had decided to become homosexual just to be fashionable, and in the process some of them went from being very scruffy to being almost too well-dressed. At the same time, some of my female friends went from being very well-dressed to wearing the clothes my previously heterosexual male friends had discarded. I found myself having to weigh up the merits of the wardrobes, and since Lisa Derbyshire looked out of this world in an old t-shirt and torn jeans it took no time at all to come to a decision.

3. How I Was Kidnapped By Brigands

I had been to a musical recital by a youthful combo called Vomit Bin and was strolling home in the light shed upon the cobbles by what I believe is called a gibbous moon. To my astonishment I was set upon by I don't know how many brigands and whisked away to an unknown location behind the local Co-op, from where they began to issue their demands, threats, and updates on social media about my general condition. They deemed my value to be far below my own estimation, and my brother paid up without having to trouble his bank. It turned out they had mistaken me for a quite well-known poet they had heard on the BBC crapping on about Yorkshire.

4. How I Kept My Cool Under Pressure

When the lads from Engineering locked me in the Pressurized Cooling Tank for a prank I thought I had had my lot. It would not be the first time one of their practical jokes had ended with the mysterious disappearance of an employee. Then I remembered my army training from a video I had once watched about army training, and thanked goodness I have a good memory, unlike my brother who took drugs back when he was young and now can't remember the words to songs he can't remember. So using the cotton wool I always carry with me, I plugged all of my orifices, imagining I would thereby be counter-balancing the weight of the outer world with the richness of my inner life. I then magically and gently deflated one of my lungs, to save air. When I regained consciousness I was stretched out on a table in the canteen, an angel choir was singing, and Betty the Tea Lady was asking me if I wanted lemon in my Earl Grey.

5. How I Married My Imaginary Girlfriend

I had the centrefold of a magazine stuck on my wall that was a picture of a young lady in green lingerie and every night she would be the last thing I saw before I fell asleep and dreamed dreams. The young lady bore a striking resemblance to the girl who worked Saturdays at the petrol station across the road from the greengrocer's where I worked Saturdays, and to whom I would cast the occasional beguiling smile when time allowed. I will skip over the fact that when I plucked up courage to ask her for a date she told me she had a boyfriend who was studying at Oxford. Forgetting her, I eventually became engaged to and then married another young lady who resembled neither the centrefold nor the petrol station girl but who, in my mind with its active imagination, surpassed both in looks, sex appeal, intelligence, and sex appeal. It was only several years later with the arrival of late-period puberty and adulthood I realized that what you see with your eyes is not necessarily what is there.

6. How I Came To Love Gruel

My wife and I had become rather affluent thanks to an accountant who knew a few tricks, and I was beginning to put on a bit of weight. The day would kick off with squid and champagne for breakfast and, since I did not actually have to work, there was not much to do during the ensuing hours, so I began to browse some books from the library pile we had been using to feed the Aga when the fire got low. That was how I came across *The Thomas Hardy Cookbook*, a very slim volume which only existed when you were so faint from hunger you began to hallucinate. And yes, I can see the contradiction.

7. How I Lost My Wife

We were holidaying on a canal boat when we were boarded by a band of pirates who ransacked our things and were more than complimentary about my wife's attractions. I was too frightened to think about disagreeing. They made me walk the plank, but as we were then navigating a very narrow stretch of the waterway I was able to step off the end of the plank on to the towpath and leg it away as fast as I could. I did not look back. I reported the outrage to the police who remarked that piracy seemed to be on the increase. I have not seen my wife since that day. I hope she is alright.

8. How I Survived Death By Boredom

It was a Thursday and so we had gone along to the regular monthly poetry reading upstairs in a store-room at H&M. I do not remember the name of the poet who was reading that night because either I never knew it or the antibiotics have not yet fully left my system. There was an open mic before the main reading but I didn't listen to that because it was an open mic. Then the main poet stepped up and began to read, and out of the window I happened to notice there was a very nice frock on display across the road in Marks & Spencer, a Jewish-stroke-British institution we would be sorry to see disappear from our local High Street, so I left very quietly to go and have a closer look.

9. How I Reorganized The World

One day I decided I was not happy with the way the world was so I decided to change some things. The flat lands I decided should be hilly, but not so hilly that they were difficult to walk at leisure. The mountains I decided could stay as they were but should be a little bit nearer to where I lived, to save on travelling. The too hot countries and the too cold countries should have the word "too" removed and replaced by "tolerably". The oceans should be rendered eternally calm, and remain plentiful of cod or haddock. As for the people, I consigned most of them to the recycle bin, except for exceptional beings including Natalie Portman and the Asian model whose name I don't know who I use as wallpaper on my laptop. I went to bed very pleased with myself for having reorganized the world, but the next morning nothing had changed because I had forgotten to press "Save", and everything had been lost when Windows 10 automatically updated during the night.

10. How I Almost Married The Manager At Lidl

I had always been an Aldi shopper but one day my friend Jed told me that the meat in Lidl was of a much higher quality and cheaper and he was right. I decided I wanted to thank the Lidl people in person so one day I asked to see the manager and he turned out to be a manageress or, as we say these days, being gender-aware, a manager. After I had spent several minutes telling she/he how much I admired her hams, how her chicken breasts were very good value, and how tasty her pork loins were, she invited me into her office where after some playful cut and thrust she said she wanted to discuss marriage and several future children, among other things.

11. How I Failed At Neighbourhood Watch

Soon after I moved in here I put my name down for the local Neighbourhood Watch scheme because I have no desire to be burgled by burglars or otherwise invaded. Long story short, on my first tour of duty I was taken in for questioning by the police as a result of the lady at number 48 phoning in to report a Peeping Tom.

12. How I Forgot Where My Family Lived

I had not seen Mum and Dad for quite a long time because I thought that when you fled the nest it was perfectly alright not to go back very often, except to pick up the occasional birthday or Christmas gift. I figured I was in very heavy arrears on the gift account, and must be owed quite a lot, so I took a coach and travelled across the several hundred miles of middle-English wilderness to pay a surprise call, Mum in particular being very fond of surprises if they did not involve anything illegal or spiritually and/or morally disturbing. It was only when a complete stranger answered the door of the house in which I had grown up I remembered that some time ago my parents had mentioned something about moving. Some people say I am too wrapped up in my own affairs to think about anyone or anything else, and use occasions like this to make their point.

THE ALLOTMENT POEMS

#1

Say all you want about carrots
But there's nothing like a young sweet one
Pulled fresh from the rich earth

#2

When the wind whips
Around the Brussels sprout plants
We are reminded of how
Often we make our own problems

#3

The difficulty of the tomato
Is not really a difficulty at all
We all of us need sun and rain
("so much depends/ upon")

It loves a house of glass

#4

Onions may give you the run-around
But you soon find out who your wife might be

#5

Courgettes may well cause arguments
But we are not children, are we? (though we love the rain)

#6

What do you mean – "Cabbages
Remind me of Russia"?

#7

So we were sitting around very much in the manner of potatoes
Suki mentioned *the coach* but she meant *the couch*

When you dig them up and the earth is under your fingernails....
What, said Suki, has that got to do with the coach?

#8

A lot of people disrespect Kale - you know
One day Kale was out shopping and Spinach just cut her
Cut her cold
What the hell?
Kale is tasty as Spinach!
I've had her
I love her
All of us in Kale City love her tasty curliness

#9

There was rhubarb in the corner of
Our patch it was there when we arrived
& it will be there when the world ends

You can't get rid of rhubarb but then
You wouldn't want to
Rhubarb crumble being the modern equivalent of Ambrosia

#10

Asparagus
A rare almost exotic delight
Occasionally
I treat myself from the organic shelf
At the supermarket –
But nurture & tend her day after day?
I am not enough of a man
Though I do, from (call it) deference,
Leave a small place
Where she could be

— What? Do you mean to say you're saying Goodbye to Creativity World, to leave, never to return?

— I have no choice. I fail who I think I am.

— But surely you will miss The Cake, and Unrestricted Sexual Adventures . . .

— I am tired of having to constantly wash myself. And water doesn't grow on trees.

— Once a Creative, always a Creative. You cannot deny that.

— The winter approaches in its duffel coat, bobble hat and mittens.

— But you still have so much to give. There can be no doubt.

— The takers of what I might have left to give are outnumbered by the fingers in a box of Cadbury's chocolate fingers. Is that an air ambulance hovering overhead? Also I find The Youth disturbing, the way they congregate at The Library since it closed down and re-opened as a hair design studio. I'm sorry – I did not mean to say so much . . . and I am apologizing to myself.

— The Youth are The Future. It says so in all the handbooks.

— The lowest common denominator keeps me awake at night. That, and the crawling.

— You are probably imagining the crawling.

— The imagination is the only reality that matters. Flocks of dogs do not look after themselves, and I am needed where they wander forlorn in fog.

— Where exactly is that?

— If you could see The Mountain it would be beyond it. But I know you cannot see even the signpost that says "To the Mountain".

— I can see what is there. I cannot see what is not there.

— We differ and diverge in so many things. I suspect your underwear is not at all like my own. And my dreams are to me what vegetables are to most people. The soil clings to their roots.

— Reference to my underwear leads me to suspect that you are not yourself. A period of bed rest and a few bowls of hot broth would do you the world of good.

— Don't send your Mother round again. I have only just had the toilet repaired.

— She loves you like a step-person.

— Keep her away from me! I am in arrears with my vaccinations. I cannot take the risk. Oh! Do you hear that?

— I hear nothing.

— It's the pirate ship coming into harbour. Black news.

— You lose me.

— I can rely only upon myself, and I fall short. Sentences have nothing in them except an emptiness that weighs more than can be held. They show no mercy!

— I repeat, you lose me.

— They have taken advantage of the tide and favourable winds. I was not expecting . . .

— I think a cup of tea might be a good idea. I shall go and put the kettle on.

— You can't go into the kitchen. It's not there any more.

— Not there?

— It wasn't happening, we were just not getting along, so I had some working class people come and take it away. Its replacement is currently being imagined, and out of bounds to anyone who doesn't have a pass.

— My questions are multiplying at an alarming rate. I can almost not keep up almost.

— I long ago found that I was unable to keep up with myself. It's been a bit of a burden.

— How did . . . ? My head is beginning to hurt . . .

— I could not keep pace with my ideas. And often I could not remember my ideas from one moment to the next. I knew they were sprouted from the seeds of genius, but I was never quick enough to pin them down before they floated away when I switched the hairdryer on. It was as if they had never been there. That was when I began to despair, and . . . oh, sorry, I'm going on a bit again.

— This is fascinating. When despair began to kick in, what did you do?

— I did nothing. There was nothing to do, at least not in any worthwhile sense. Fortunately this awful city has a number of easy-to-find sex gyms and opium dens, and there is always a bar open somewhere. Listen! I hear cutlasses being drawn from their scabbards. The pirates are at the door! The blackness has blackened further.

— I cannot hear anything.

— Hush!

—

— It's alright. I think they have passed by. They will be headed for the university campus, where there are rich pickings. Pedants, wastrels, creative writing students, and one or two alleged virgins. I was saying about how I should have paid more attention to establishing myself as a brand . . .

— I don't ...

— I should have paid more attention to establishing myself as a brand, like *Cillit Bang* or *I Can't Believe It's Not Butter*. People like brands. Brands do people's thinking for them.

—

— *Armitage Shanks* is a brand, and look how far that has come from humble beginnings as a basic receptacle and in possession of limited talents. Half the world pisses and poops into it, and *Armitage Shanks* laughs all the way to the bank. But it doesn't matter. I no longer rely on words.

— What do you mean?

— I am snow. Or I am the slush that snow becomes and that children look at with dismay. I am long-distance envisioning. I am cold, but that might be because the central heating is broken. I am unseen environmental changes. I am universal liberal concern that somehow can't be bothered. But I survive. That I have failed myself can be accepted. That I am able to walk into a magical pantry of my own making is beyond people's comprehension, and the feasts that await me will be like balm for the think-pan. There is more than one way to skin a, I hesitate to say "cat" because I love cats, shall we say "whale" instead? There is more than one way to skin a whale. I may have to edit that . . . I am saying more than I had planned to say. I think I will cut out my tongue. Please hand me a scalpel.

A NOTE TO THE POEMS

Moby-Dick has long been one my favourite novels (or non-novels, as the poem has it). I came to it rather late, and although I have read it perhaps four or five times I've not read it enough. As for the poem, well, for me the most interesting poems to write (and probably to read) are those whose genesis is mysterious and that insist upon existing without much planning or preparation. So a title or an idea might suddenly pop into my head, and away we go.... In this case, the title appeared and, not long after, the idea of narrating a kind of marathon readathon came to me. So the poem begins at the beginning of Chapter One with a very corny play on 'Call me Ishmael', and then proceeds in somewhat random steps through the book, quoting and tweaking quotations and incorporating my own sometimes but not always relevant thoughts, and events from the everyday. It was composed over the course of several days, days when I would often, as the poem says, get up 'with nothing to say but a great urge to say it.' Of course, there is usually something to say, but it is not always worth saying. Now, almost four years after writing the poem, I'm not always sure exactly which words are mine and which are Melville's. Often it's obvious but sometimes it's not. The poem is not about anything in particular, it just is. I like poems like that.

As for the other poems here, a good deal of "Preces: Contemplating Mrs. Baxter " is from Thomas Merton's "New Seeds of Contemplation", a book I know for a fact Mrs. Baxter has not read, and all of the highlights from "The Art of Translation" were found online, in translations of Chinese poems into what the translators evidently thought was English. I have taken the liberty of (a) stealing the various lines from here and there and (b) organizing them into what appear to be poems, but aren't really. And, as can be seen by the presence of quotation marks, each of the poems in the "View" sequence include a quotation. I can remember where some of them come from, but mostly not. I'm sure there are other bits of other texts scattered throughout the book, especially in the extracts from "What Matters", but again, I can't remember what they are or where they came from.

— April 2020

Martin Stannard was the founding editor of *joe soap's canoe* (1978-1993), a poetry magazine some people regard as legendary. He also acted (the correct word) as poetry editor of the online art and poetry magazine *Decals of Desire*. Other stuff could be said, but trying to condense 40-odd years in Poetry World ('odd' is also the correct word) would be either (a) pointless or (b) tedious or (c) both. In 2007-8 he was the Royal Literary Fund Writing Fellow at Nottingham Trent University but, that year aside, he taught English, Literature and Culture at a university in China from 2005 until 2018, when he returned to the UK to witness it self-destruct first-hand.

website: http://www.martinstannard.com/
joe soap's canoe can be found archived at http://www.martinstannard.com/jsc/jschome.html

Decals of Desire: http://decalsofdesire.blogspot.com/

Some other titles by Martin Stannard:

The Review
The Moon is About 238,855 Miles Away (Versions after the Chinese)
Items
Poems for the Young at Heart
Respondings (online)
How to Live a Life (online)
Faith
Coral
Difficulties and Exultations
Writing Down the Days
Poems on Various Subjects
Conversations with Myself
A Hundred of Happiness
Easter
From a Recluse to a-Roving I Will Go
The Gracing of Days

Here is a major book by a major British poet who dances in the ballroom where the avant-garde meets the mainstream and, more importantly, makes us all want to dance there too. In Martin Stannard's hands language is never tired, or threadbare, or past its sell-by date or begrudging or lightweight.

— **Ian McMillan**, back cover blurb for *Poems for the Young at Heart*

You can never, it used to be (rightly) said, open Tennyson on the wrong page. The same applies to Stannard . . . (He) is not only an intoxicatingly entertaining poet; here he proves himself one with the emotional assurance and the artistry to strike (after exquisitely delicate preparation) the seriously subjective note.

— **D.M. de Silva**, at *Poetry Salzburg Review* on *Poems for the Young at Heart*

In the final song of Gustav Mahler's *Das Lied von der Erde* (1909), *'Der Abschied,'* ('The Farewell'), the contralto sings the words: *'I seek peace for my lonely heart.'* The words could easily stand as the motto for Martin Stannard's . . . *The Moon Is About 238,855 Miles Away*, a beautiful collection of 'Versions after the Chinese.'

— **Jonathan Taylor**, at *Litter* on *The Moon Is About 238,855 Miles Away*

The poems Martin Stannard writes now still very much possess all the appealing qualities of his earlier poems, without, however, being in any way repetitious. His work is informed by, among others, the Romantics, the Surrealists and the New York poets (with shades of Koch, O'Hara and Ashbery), but the poems he writes are instantly recognizable as his. It is a poetry which should be much, much more widely-known than it is at present.

— **Ian Seed**, at *Tears in the Fence*, on *Items*

www.ingramcontent.com/pod-product-compliance
Lightning Source LLC
Chambersburg PA
CBHW081140090426
42736CB00018B/3422

* 9 7 8 1 9 9 9 9 4 5 1 5 2 *